Our World of Water

Lakes

Arthur Best

New York

Published in 2018 by Cavendish Square Publishing, LLC
243 5th Avenue, Suite 136, New York, NY 10016

Cataloging-in-Publication Data

Names: Best, Arthur, author.
Title: Lakes / Arthur Best.
Description: New York : Cavendish Square, 2018. | Series: Our world of water | Includes index.
Identifiers: ISBN 9781502630902 (pbk.) | ISBN 9781502630933 (library bound) | ISBN 9781502630919 (6 pack) | ISBN 9781502630926 (ebook)
Subjects: LCSH: Lakes--Juvenile literature.
Classification: LCC GB1603.8 B47 2018 | DDC 551.48'2--dc23

Editorial Director: David McNamara
Copy Editor: Nathan Heidelberger
Associate Art Director: Amy Greenan
Designer: Alan Sliwinski
Production Coordinator: Karol Szymczuk
Photo Research: J8 Media

Printed in the United States of America

Contents

Lakes are **bodies** of water.

Lakes are **inland**.

There is land between lakes and the sea.

Lakes can be small.

They can also be huge!

Lake Superior is the largest lake in North America.

Lakes usually have freshwater.

You could drink the water.

Lakes get their water
from rain.

The rain falls on land that
is close by.

Streams and rivers take the
rain to the lake.

10

11

Water can leave the lake through a river or stream.

Water can also **evaporate**.

The sun heats the water.

The water turns to steam you can't see.

13

Many plants grow in lakes.

Seaweed grows in lakes.

Water lilies grow in lakes.

Cattails grow in lakes.

15

Fish live in lakes.

Minnows are small fish that live in lakes.

Sturgeons are some of the biggest lake fish.

17

Lots of other animals
need lakes.

Turtles and crayfish live
in lakes.

Ducks float on lakes.

Frogs live near lakes.

18

Animals need clean water to drink.

So do people!

We need to keep our lakes clean.

Everyone needs good water!

New Words

bodies (BAH-deez) Complete areas.

evaporate (e-VA-puh-rayt) Turn to steam.

inland (IN-land) Away from the sea.

minnows (MIH-nohs) Some small fish.

sturgeons (STIR-juns) Some very large fish.

Index

About the Author

Arthur Best lives in Wisconsin with his wife and son. He has written many other books for children. His house is close to a lake.

About BOOKWORMS

Bookworms help independent readers gain reading confidence through high-frequency words, simple sentences, and strong picture/text support. Each book explores a concept that helps children relate what they read to the world they live in.